Where in the World?

Laaren Brown

D0645301

SCHOLASTIC INC.

New York Toronto London Auckland
Sydney Mexico City New Delhi Hong Kong

Read more! Do more!

After you read this book, download your free all-new digital activities.

You can show what a great reader you are!

Where in the World?
reading fun

enter

For Mac and PC

Play games and do activities with videos and sounds!

True or false?

see   draw   home

Where in the World? true or false?

Where in the World? true or false?

Where in the World? true or false?

Make a landmarks map
Stick famous landmarks on a map of the world.
Include the ones in your book. Find out about others, too!

back   home

You will need . . .
A pencil

Now click the numbers . . .
1 2 3

Log on to
www.scholastic.com/ discovermore/readers
Enter this special code:
L3P29TGPD4P3

Contents

ISBN 978-0-545-63639-1

12 11 10 9 8 7 6 5 4 3   14 15 16 17 18 19/0

Printed in the U.S.A. 40
This edition first printing, April 2014

Where in the world?

Let's take a trip around the world. Let's go and see the most amazing landmarks on Earth. Landmarks are famous buildings or structures. They tell us about the people who built them and how they lived their lives. Some landmarks were homes to kings and emperors. Some protected their

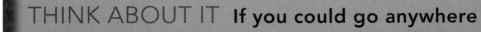

THINK ABOUT IT **If you could go anywhere**

countries from enemies. Some were built to remember important people who had died. Landmarks tell us about what was important to the people who built them. They tell us what those people valued most. They make the people in their countries proud.

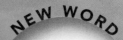
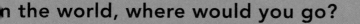

The Americas

Your trip starts on a little island in New York Harbor. Look up at the Statue of Liberty, a gift to the United States from France. It was meant to say, "You love liberty, and we love liberty, too!"

> **Dr. Alan Kraut, Ellis Island Foundation**
>
> Here's a statue that stands right at the entry of the country you're coming to, and it represents freedom.

The lady with the torch lights the way to Ellis Island. For more than 30 years, people from all around the world entered the United States there. The statue is a symbol of the US, the land of the free.

Come on in!

Between 1851 and 1910, about 25 million people entered the US, at Ellis Island and other places.

2,598,000	2,315,000	2,812,000	5,147,000	3,688,000	8,795,000
1851–1860	1861–1870	1871–1880	1881–1890	1891–1900	1901–1910

Travel west 1,725 miles (2,776 km) and you'll arrive at Mount Rushmore, in the Black Hills of South Dakota. In 1927, work began on a grand project there. Sculptor Gutzon Borglum organized 400 workers.

George Washington (president 1789–1797)

Thomas Jefferson (president 1801–1809)

Mount Rushmore before carving began

George Washington, almost finished

Workers carving in hanging chairs

Wow

Work on a secret cave room

They blasted away tons of rock with dynamite, then carved giant faces. Today, four US presidents stare out from the rock. What made these four so special? They all had big ideas for the US, and they made those ideas come to life. Mount Rushmore inspires Americans to work together to make the US great.

Theodore Roosevelt (president 1901–1909)

Abraham Lincoln (president 1861–1865)

behind the faces was started but never finished.

Moving west over the Rocky Mountains, you'll find the huge and awe-inspiring Hoover Dam. Not only is it beautiful, but it works hard, too! The dam helps control the flow of the Colorado River. It uses the flow to make electricity. It produces all the energy needed by 1.3 million people in California, Nevada, and Arizona.

Water flows
into towers.

Hoover Dam

Hoover
Dam

Water is
piped into
turbines.

Colorado
River

Building the dam in the 1930s was a massive effort. Many people said it couldn't be done! But Herbert Hoover, the 31st president, backed the project and work started on the dam. It is one of the largest structures in the world and is visited by more than 1 million people a year.

INSIDE A TURBINE

Wires carry the electricity to towns and cities...

Water makes the turbines spin. That produces electricity.

Now take a trip to Peru, in South America. You can climb so high, it feels like you're touching the Sun! At Machu Picchu, in the Andes Mountains, lie the ruins of an amazing palace. Almost 600 years ago, the palace was full of life. It was built for an emperor so that he could be close to the Sun.

To the Inca people, the emperor wasn't just a ruler. He was a god. So he needed a place to relax that was like the home of the gods.

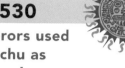

TIME LINE

1450

The Inca emperor ordered his workers to build Machu Picchu.

1455–1530

Inca emperors used Machu Picchu as a summer palace.

1524–1526

Two-thirds of the Inca people died from a disease.

1532

Spanish soldiers invaded Peru, searching for gold. They made the Incas slaves.

1530s

Machu Picchu was abandoned. The Spanish never found it.

1911

American Hiram Bingham discovered the ruins of Machu Picchu.

Europe

Start your visit to Europe in Italy. Rome is the capital of Italy. In its busy center stand the remains of the Colosseum. The ancient Romans built this giant sports arena. The most popular events were gladiator fights. Up to 75,000 fans could pack into the arena. They watched gladiators fight to the death!

NEW WORD

In ancient Rome, **gladiators** (GLAD-ee-ay-turs) were trained to fight in arenas.

SAY IT OUT LOUD

Parthenon

Travel east to Greece. The Parthenon is one of the most beautiful ancient buildings of all. The ancient Greeks built it for Athena, their goddess of wisdom.

GLADIATOR FIGHTS

Weapons

Gladiators learned to fight in special schools. Then they usually fought to the death.

Trident

Dagger

Net

Battles

Sometimes gladiators had big battles. They fought one another from chariots drawn by horses.

Wild animals

Lions and tigers were kept in pens under the arena. They were brought up to fight the gladiators.

Make sure to stop in London, the capital city of England. Towering over the River Thames is a mighty castle. A king built the Tower of London in about 1100, to show his power. Later, part of it became a dark and terrible prison. Many important people were kept there.

DEATHS AT THE TOWER

Anne Boleyn

One of the six wives of King Henry VIII, Anne was beheaded in 1536.

Catherine Howard

Catherine was another of Henry VIII's wives! He had her beheaded in 1542

Some were tortured. Some were put to death. Today, the tower is guarded by special soldiers called Beefeaters. Six ravens also live there. It is said that if the number of ravens drops below six, the tower—and England—will fall.

Lady Jane Grey
Queen of England for only nine days, she was beheaded in 1554.

Robert Devereux
He led an army against Queen Elizabeth I. He was beheaded in 1601.

Imagine this: You're in Paris, France, and it's March 31, 1889. You're going to be the first person to climb the Eiffel Tower! The elevators aren't ready yet. So Gustave Eiffel, the tower's designer, leads you up the stairs. You climb and climb . . . until at last you stand 906 feet (276 m) above Paris. Soon the French flag is snapping in the breeze. You watch a happy crowd celebrate far below. The tallest landmark in Paris is open!

EIFFEL TOWER BY THE NUMBERS

Paint used: 66 tons, every 7 years

Height: 1,063 feet (324 m)

Weight: 11,133 tons

August 1887

March 1888

September 1888

Number of rivets: 2,500,000
Number of metal parts: 18,000

Number of elevators: 7, traveling 64,000 miles (103,000 km) per year

Number of steps to the top: 1,665

Where else in the world?

You are standing on hot desert sand near Cairo, in Egypt. Raise your eyes. You will see an enormous pyramid soaring above you. The Great Pyramid is the only remaining Wonder of the Ancient World. It was built about 4,600 years ago. It was a tomb for a king named Khufu.

Each side is 755 feet (230 m) long.

INSIDE THE GREAT PYRAMID

Khufu's burial chamber

Air shaft

Underground room

Wow

When it was first built, the

The Great Pyramid is made of
2.3 million blocks of heavy stone. It
was the tallest building in the world
for nearly 4,000 years.

Great Pyramid (right), with two
other ancient pyramids nearby

The stones
were dragged
and pushed
up a ramp.

Workers lived on the site.

Great Pyramid was over 480 feet (146 m) high.

Thousands of miles to the east, you will reach the Great Wall of China. This is the longest structure on Earth. The first emperor of China built it to protect his empire. When you stand on it, you can imagine that you are a Chinese soldier keeping a lookout.

The widest section of the wall is 30 feet (9 m). It is said that one worker died for every foot of its length. Today, some sections are in ruins.

In 2012, Chinese experts showed that the Great Wall is 13,170 miles (21,195 km) long. That's more than twice as long as people once thought it was!

Stretched out, the wall would reach halfway around the world.

It's four times as long as the United States is wide.

It's as long as 2,395 Mount Everests, stacked on top of one another, are tall.

It's the same length as 7,728,366 people holding hands . . .

. . . or 662,412 blue whales, nose to tail.

Once upon a time, there was an emperor in northern India who loved his wife very much. But she died. The emperor was so sad that he built a beautiful marble tomb, the Taj Mahal. From the outside, everyone could see the gleaming dome. Four minarets stood at the four corners. Inside, it was decorated with rich and colorful gems.

NEW WORD

A **minaret** (min-uh-RET) is a tower or turret from which people are called to prayer.

SAY IT OUT LOUD

This is the true love story of Shah Jahan and his beloved wife Mumtaz Mahal. She died in 1631. It took 22,000 workers 22 years to build her magnificent tomb in the city of Agra. When the shah died in 1666, his body was placed inside, alongside his wife's. The Taj Mahal reminds us to think of those we love and those we have lost.

Shah Jahan and Mumtaz Mahal

Your world tour ends in another harbor. This one is in Australia. You are on the other side of the world from New York, where you started. What do you think of the Sydney Opera House? Does it look like a sailing ship to you? Or like the wings of a bird?

There are over 1 million tiles on the roof. Each section of roof weighs up to 15 tons. The bridge, hundreds of boats, and the glittering water are spread out before you. It's one of the most beautiful sights in the world. It's a great place to end your journey.

Where to next?

Montreal Biosphere

Visitors flock to this science museum in Canada. They can walk around its giant dome. It is 249 feet (76 m) wide and 203 feet (62 m) high!

McMurdo Station

This is a US research station in Antarctica. More than 1,000 people live and work there. It is the largest "town" in Antarctica.

Nelson Mandela

Robben Island

The jail on this island off South Africa is famous. This is because of one prisoner—the freedom fighter Nelson Mandela. He was freed in 1990 after 27 years.

THINK ABOUT IT **Why are the landmarks o**

Millau Viaduct

This bridge in southern France is the tallest bridge in the world. It is 1,125 feet (343 m) high! It crosses the valley of the Tarn River.

United Nations Headquarters

The United Nations (UN) was formed in 1945. It aims to keep peace between all countries. Its building is in New York City. More than 1 million people visit it each year.

Burj Khalifa

This skyscraper in Dubai is the tallest man-made structure in the world. It is 2,717 feet (828 m) from ground to top.

Glossary

abandon
To leave something behind and never go back.

ancient
Very old, or from long ago.

arena
A large area or building used for sports and fun.

Beefeater
A special soldier who guards the Tower of London.

behead
To kill someone by cutting off his or her head.

chariot
A small vehicle with two wheels, pulled by horses.

dam
A barrier built across a river to control its flow.

disease
A sickness that spreads from person to person.

dome
A large round roof.

dynamite
A material that explodes, used to blast rock apart.

electricity
A type of energy that powers lights and machines.

emperor
The male ruler of an empire, or kingdom.

gladiator
A person trained to fight in arenas in ancient Rome.

harbor
An area of water near land, where boats can stop safely.

Inca
A member of a South American Indian people who lived in Peru from about 1100 to the early 1530s.

landmark
A building or structure that is very important to people.

liberty
Freedom.

minaret
A tower or turret from which people are called to prayer.

pyramid
A tomb built by ancient Egyptians. A pyramid has sides shaped like triangles.

ramp
A sloping surface that joins two surfaces at different levels.

raven
A type of large black bird.

rivet
A metal pin that holds two pieces of metal together.

sculptor
A person who makes art by carving or shaping stone, wood, or metal.

slave
A person who is owned by another person.

tomb
A building or room for holding a dead body.

turbine
A machine with blades that are moved by water, wind, or gas.

viaduct
A bridge that carries a road or railroad over a valley.

Index

Images
Alamy Images: 26 main, 27 (BL Images Ltd.), 25 inset (Dinodia Photos), 8 tl (Everett Collection Historical), 28 bl (Friedrich von Horsten/Images of Africa Photobank), 15 rc (Henry Wismayer), 8 tc, 17 br (INTERFOTO), 17 inset (Peter Phipp/Travelshots.com), 10 inset (Radek Hofman), 28 cr (William Sutton/DanitaDelimont.com); Dreamstime: back cover (Aladin66), cover bg globes (Artman), 16 bg, 17 bg (Chrisdorney), cover tl (Dan Breckwoldt), 6 main, 7 main (Kenishirotie), 32 (Lowerkase), cover lct (Martin A. Graf), cover lcb (Miketanct), cover main (Sumners Graphics Inc.), cover br (Witr); Getty Images: 19 tl (De Agostini Picture Library), 16 br (Hans the Younger Holbein/The Bridgeman Art Library), 21 b inset (Manuel ROMARÍS), 19 tc, 19 tr (Roger Viollet/Hulton Archive), 28 bc (Tom Stoddart Archive); iStockphoto: 2 camel (jane), 16 spot (pictore), 7 b (ziggymaj); Library of Congress/Rise Studio, Rapid City, S. Dak.: 8 tr; Scholastic, Inc.: inside front cover silos, 8 b, 13 clock, 13 all other time line images, 20 b, 23 all other images; Shutterstock, Inc.: 4 bl (AG-PHOTO), 15 net (Aigars Reinholds), 4 br (Aleksandar Mijatovic), 29 tr (Alexander Ryabintsev), 5 tl (Alexander Studentschnig), 15 dagger (Ana Martinez de Mingo), 19 bl (Andrey_Kuzmin), 5 tr (Anton_Ivanov), 28 cl, 29 br (astudio), 24 bg border, 25 bg border (clearviewstock), 2 bg, 3 bg (Dan Breckwoldt), 30, 31 (DOPhoto), 28 tr, 28 br, 29 cl (ducu59us), 15 br (ehtesham), 15 bl (Eric Isselee), 5 bl (Galyna Andrushko), 17 bl (Georgios Kollidas), cover tr, 22 bg, 23 l (Hung Chung Chih), 14 main, 15 l bg (Iakov Kalinin), cover rcb (ivan bastien), 4 t (Jane Rix), 19 br (JPL Designs), 4 bc (Justin Black), 18 bl (Karramba Production), 12 main, 13 l (Lukasz Kurbiel), 7 t, 9 inset, 11 inset, 12 inset, 14 inset, 15 globe, 16 t inset, 18 inset, 21 t inset, 22 t inset, 24 inset, 26 inset (Maisei Raman), 16 c inset (Marina Jay), 28 tl (meunierd), 4 t bg, 5 t bg (mexrix), 29 tl (Migel), 5 br (Mikadun), 19 bc (motodan), 6 inset, 28 inset, 29 inset (nahariyani), 15 tl (Nick Pavlakis), 2 plane (Perfect Gui), 18 bg, 19 bg (r.nagy), 10 t bg, 11 t bg (rotofrank), 13 rct (sahua d), cover rct, 24 bg main, 25 bg main (saiko3p), 8 bg, 9 main (Shu-Hung Liu), 29 cr (Steve Broer), 18 br (Stocksnapper), 29 bl (SurangaSL), 22 b inset (Tan Kian Khoon), 15 trident (Thorsten Rust), 18 bc (Yulia Glam), 1 main (Zack Frank), cover bl; Tim Loughhead/Precision Illustration: 10 main, 11 main, 20 main, 21 bg.